"*Things You Think About When You Bite Your Nails* is a tender and witty examination of fear, in which Amalia Andrade shows us that fear is as universal and useful a teacher as heartbreak. She gives us an empowering opportunity to be observers of our own anxieties, and therefore become better caretakers of them. By the end of this funny, compassionate, and interactive deep dive into the things that scare us, I was ready to ask my fears to dance! During an era when the unknown future seems especially frightening, this book is a must-have companion that reminds us how much power we actually have over our own lives."
—Mari Andrew, author of *Am I There Yet?* and *My Inner Sky*

"Amalia Andrade is back with another book packed full of kindhearted, relatable, slightly manic, pop-culture-infused personal insight and reflective prompts. Deeply human, this book on fear and anxiety has already touched many like-minded souls and is sure to continue its impact with this English translation."
—Adam J. Kurtz, artist and author of *1 Page at a Time*

"*Things You Think About When You Bite Your Nails* is a comforting, humorous, and unique endeavor into demystifying fear. Amalia Andrade so cleverly explores universal truths behind anxiety, while making room for the reader's own terrifying thoughts."
—Jordan Sondler, author of *Feel It Out*

"As a fellow artist, I can certainly say that I hate Amalia. I'm deeply envious of her vulnerability, and her clever ability to make me confront my own fears and traumas, all while making me laugh. Can you believe the nerve?! If you're interested in rediscovering yourself, or just laughing hard, please read this book and hate-love her along with me."
—Timothy Goodman, author of *Sharpie Art Workshop*

"This book is a comprehensive tool kit wrapped up in a soft warm blanket. It gives you the courage to fight your darkest fears, and it offers you the comfort to quieten your loudest anxieties. It is a safe and supportive space that will encourage you to live a fear-free life. Most of all, this book succeeds where most self-help books fail; it actually helps."
—Lee Crutchley, author of *How to Be Happy (Or at Least Less Sad)*

AMALIA ANDRADE

THINGS YOU THINK ABOUT WHEN YOU BITE YOUR NAILS

A FEAR AND ANXIETY WORKBOOK

life

PENGUIN BOOKS

An imprint of Penguin Random House LLC
penguinrandomhouse.com

LIBRARY OF CONGRESS CATALOGING-IN-PUBLICATION DATA
Names: Andrade, Amalia, 1986– author.
Title: Things you think about when you bite your nails : a fear and anxiety workbook / Amalia Andrade.
Identifiers: LCCN 2020024761 (print) | LCCN 2020024762 (ebook) | ISBN 9780143134916 (trade paperback) | ISBN 9780525506584 (ebook)
Subjects: LCSH: Fear. | Nail-biting. | Emotions.
Classification: LCC BF575.F2 A453 2020 (print) | LCC BF575.F2 (ebook) | DDC 152.4/6--dc23
LC record available at https://lccn.loc.gov/2020024761
LC ebook record available at https://lccn.loc.gov/2020024762

First published in Spanish as *Cosas que piensas cuando te muerdes las uñas* by Espasa, an imprint of Editorial Planeta Colombiana S.A., Bogotá, Colombia

Printed in the United States of America

1 3 5 7 9 10 8 6 4 2

Set in Chaparral Pro

Designed by Amalia Andrade and Sabrina Bowers

FOR SANTIAGO,
BECAUSE LOVE IS
GREATER THAN FEAR

WARNING

This book is full of drawings and words of encouragement and gentleness. But it is also about fear. I know that sometimes neither illustrations nor soft words are able to diminish fear's power. That's why it is important for me to share that this book may have images or words that may be triggering for some readers. Inside these pages I talk about clowns, falling airplanes, uncles dying alone because of their fear of loneliness. I talk about syringes, dentists, spiders, witchcraft, failure, and darkness. I also talk about mental health, anxiety disorders, post-traumatic stress, phobia management, and OCD.

This book will ask you to kindly confront your fears. It is only through gentle and direct confrontation that fears can be overcome. The only way out is through.

I felt a cleaving in my mind
As if my brain had split;
I tried to match it, seam by seam,
But could not make them fit.

— EMILY DICKINSON

I write as though to save
someone's life. Probably my own.

— CLARICE LISPECTOR,
   A Breath of Life

CONTENTS

INTRODUCTION

BUT WHY A BOOK ABOUT FEAR ?

Dear reader, this is a book about fear—and as such, it's very likely that while reading it you will experience some moments of terror. This doesn't mean that this is a SCARY BOOK. There are no monsters here. Actually, yes, there are some. But their purpose isn't to scare you. Their purpose is to help you unmask your fears, to take power from them, to conquer them.

This book is like stepping into a Freddy Krueger movie and, instead of being brutally murdered in your sleep, realizing that Freddy is actually a lowly modern-day adult who has to fill out his W-9 and pay his bills again because his payment bounced (for the tenth time), who has just been dumped by his boyfriend, and who suffers from post-traumatic stress disorder from that time his brother—on accident—dumped boiling hot tea on his face when he was thirteen years old, forever ruining his dream of starring in telenovelas.

None of this justifies Freddy's murder attempts—what I mean is that Freddy is most likely a sociopath and should probably go see a psychiatrist—but after learning all of this he doesn't seem quite so scary, right? Okay, fine, yes, he's still a little bit scary, but now that we understand him we think, "Poor Freddy, all he ever wanted was to be a telenovela hunk."

Well, that understanding is what's going to happen with this book—not understanding Freddy Krueger, dear reader, but rather understanding your inexplicable fear of rats or your fear of loneliness and rejection.

Fear can either be your ally or your enemy, depending on how well you understand it and on whether it controls you or you control it. In my case, I decided to write this book because, as time went on, my personal list of fears began to grow at an uncontrollable pace. I wanted to understand how I went from being a girl capable of eating sand straight out of the children's sandbox (I know, this is gross; don't ask) to being a young adult (this term makes me feel less old) incapable of touching the door of a public bathroom without suffering a small panic attack* thinking about the possibility of catching a deadly virus.

---

* In my case, my fear turned into a profound anxiety that completely consumed me, slowly but surely. (For more information on fear spiraling out of control, see Chapter 4.)

THIS IS ME, PERFECTLY CALM
ON THE OUTSIDE WHILE
SCREAMING ON THE INSIDE
AND DYING OF ANXIETY
AT THE SAME TIME

A BRIEF HISTORY OF MY OWN FEARS

Throughout my life, my fear has worn many different masks. For years, it made itself known through horrible asthma. During the very worst times, I could barely breathe. As a kid my mouth always tasted like albuterol, like medicine, like the urge to cry. I'd chew gum, but the taste would linger, stagnant. I'd pilfer pastries. I'd sneak the grape-flavored popsicles that Jenny—my nanny—would buy for me at the corner store after I'd promise that I would eat all my soup, I would be well-behaved, I wouldn't bite her when I got angry for no reason—because that's what I was like.

(I don't remember biting her, but Jenny shows me the scars on her back, the marks of my teeth in irregular shapes—like warm-water lakes—embedded in her skin, and says: "The more I'd ask you to stop, the harder you'd bite."

"Like a crocodile," I say, laughing.

But Jenny doesn't laugh.)

I remember waking up many nights and walking to Mom's room, filled with fear from my nightmares or overcome by the need to make sure she hadn't died in her sleep. The asthma attacks didn't strike in the moment—instead, they would come two or three days later, out of nowhere, for no reason, while I slept or read a book or played in the pool with my brother, pretending to be aquatic detectives or rulers of the ocean.

I didn't understand that my asthma was a mask for my anxiety until I stopped having asthma altogether and the fear stuck around, growing inside me.

As I grew older, the monster transformed into a fear of vomiting. I remember particular moments, like the time I woke up abruptly and threw up all over my Disney Pocahontas rug. I ran to Mom's room wailing, "Mom, I threw up!" as though it was the most gruesome thing that could happen to anyone, feeling like both a culprit and a victim of some horrible crime. I became consumed with the fear that I'd throw up again and turned to elaborate rituals—refusing to sleep on my side, sticking my head out the window of the school bus to avoid troubling smells, guzzling Alka-Seltzer in secret—to ensure it would never happen again.

It wasn't until a few years later, when reading *Bart Simpson's Guide to Life* (a book that was foundational for me throughout my teenage years), that I discovered my fear wasn't just fear but a phobia that had a name: emetophobia. The tangled mess of darkness living inside me had a name, and that meant it existed outside of me, beyond me. I wasn't alone!

A phobia is rarely what it seems on the surface. Often, it's a disguise for deeper and stronger fears, for unprocessed emotions that find a way to escape our bodies by turning into something else. My emetophobia isn't simply a fear of vomiting—it's a fear of losing control, of falling apart, of being violently vulnerable. In time, I came to understand this. But not without first spending too much time locked inside a prison I built for myself, one wrought not of iron bars but of evasion, rituals, manias, and compulsions.

Whether it's my childhood fears of asthma attacks and vomiting, or more recent fears like the thought of going crazy or dying in a plane crash, my fear has worn many masks and dressed up as many things. It has stayed with me, like an enigmatic companion who is difficult to understand. Maybe as a survival mechanism. Maybe as an antiquated biological response. Maybe because of my inherited genetics. Maybe as a friend, one who could teach me lessons about courage and leaps of faith. Or maybe for no reason at all.

Fear is tricky, and it is so hard to overcome. That is why, when I found myself at age twenty-seven, cornered in the sterile and antiseptic office of an unknown psychiatrist who looked at me with both pity and concern, I thought it was too late. The psychiatrist explained to me, "You have generalized anxiety disorder amplified by panic disorder with agoraphobia, as well as specific phobia disorder," and prescribed me medication that would take two weeks to start working. "You're probably not going to feel great at first, but that's normal," she told me. "It'll get better soon."

She was clearly being optimistic when she said "soon" and "not great." I felt like I was dying. But I made it.

I don't know where I found the strength. It came from parts of me I had never known before, not because they were invisible but because I had never tried to acknowledge their existence. I managed to drag myself up and out of bed, trying to put the pieces of my life back together after every line had blurred. I went to the psychiatrist's once a week, every week, for five months.

I came to understand that to feel is to heal. And so, I embraced my torments without shame. I felt the pain I had swallowed as a child all over my skin. I pushed through the things that hurt me cruelly, delicately, meticulously. I looked them in the eye. I didn't avoid any part of them; instead, I roamed their every corner, and I healed. The anxiety disappeared, the darkness lifted from my chest, and I was once again able to recognize the different shapes and pieces of my life.

"It's time to give new meaning to my life," I said in one of those sessions. And my psychologist told me: "Write that down and hang it on the wall." I said I would, but I didn't.

Instead, I wrote this book.

WHAT YOU'LL FIND IN THIS BOOK

In this book, I'm going to explore fear: the ins and outs, its complexities, its character, how it disguises itself so easily. To understand fear, we need to unmask it, and so the whole purpose of this book is to help you do exactly that. We live in an age where fear is always lurking around the corner like a creepy entity, but I think we can invite it into the light, make it a little less creepy.

In the following chapters, you'll learn about the origins of your fears, as well as how to talk to them and navigate them. You'll also find a chapter where I explore what it means when fear spirals out of control as an anxiety disorder, how to identify what is happening to you, and how to cope with it in successful ways.

Throughout, I'm going to ask you to draw or write your fears, because drawing or writing your fears helps you become conscious of them, and becoming conscious of them helps you articulate them, and articulating them is important because, as Stephen King said, "If a fear cannot be articulated, it can't be conquered."

Dedicating ourselves to profoundly examining our fears can be an intimidating, at times painful, and without a doubt very scary task. But we are NEVER alone in fear. On the following pages, you will find contributions from my brilliant artist and writer friends that I've called Support Group so that you never forget that you don't have to go through fear alone. We got you.

Ready? Good. Let's start with a quick test. . . . .

FEAR
SELF-ASSESSMENT
TEST

This test will help you understand what level of fear you deal with on a daily basis according to a Richter scale of fears.

NOTE: *The Richter scale of fears was invented by me and has nothing to do with the seismologist Charles Francis Richter (despite the fact that earthquakes and panic attacks can feel like the same thing).*

1. Which of these three images is scarier to you?

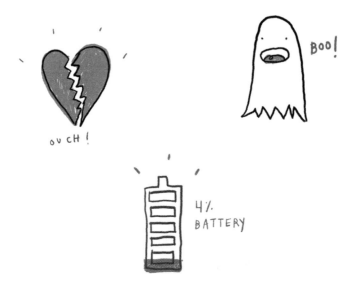

2. Do you live in fear of one of the following things?

    a. Being alone forever and never finding the love of your life (or finding them and then losing them)
    b. Dying without ever having achieved your dreams
    c. Sending a screenshot to the wrong person
    d. Waking up to find twenty missed calls from your mother in the middle of the night
    e. All of the above
    f. Feeling like nothing will ever be done to end climate change, increasing the probability of the human race dying due to a storm of biblical proportions (or something of the sort)

3. Have you ever chosen to stay in a job or relationship that was bad for you because you feared uncertainty or/and that you would never find something better?

   a. Yes
   b. No
   c. I think I have, but I'm too embarrassed to admit it to myself.

4. Loneliness is:

   a. A song by the Police
   b. My great-aunt's name
   c. The most terrifying thing on earth
   d. A state of plentitude
   e. Something that doesn't scare me or even exist since Netflix was invented

5. Consider the following scenario:

   > Once upon a time, there was a young man named Arthur who quit his job as director of operations at a sticker company—where he had guaranteed Social Security and an indefinite-term contract—in order to chase his dream of becoming an astrology guru on the internet. After putting everything into his dream, Arthur failed (partially because he knew nothing about social media and partially because in the middle of it all he realized he wasn't really passionate about the subject) and was left with nothing. He had to move back to his parents' place with his dog, Cindy (named after Cindy Crawford, of course), and start over from scratch.

   > What level of fear does this spark in you?

   a. Fear
   b. Lots of fear
   c. No fear at all
   d. TERROR

6. Which of these is scariest?

   a. Falling in love
   b. Falling out of love
   c. Success
   d. Failure
   e. Growing up
   f. Your accountant's face
   g. ALL OF THE ABOVE

7. Pick a scenario straight from your nightmares:

   a. Speaking in public
   b. Going to the dentist every day
   c. Being in a plane crash
   d. Getting one hundred shots in a single visit to the doctor
   e. Needing to call your cable/internet provider who is unable to solve ANYTHING, EVER, making you feel like you're going mad
   f. Being governed by authoritarian leaders who make the world feel like a horror movie and/or the world ending due to incompetent leaders

RESULTS

No matter what answers you picked, most likely you are somewhat afraid. Or you're very, very afraid. Whatever your level of fear, it's okay; you are definitely not alone. While some people might be more conscious of their fears than others, everyone has them. What's crucial is that you learn to articulate those fears, confront them, and live with them.

The easiest fears to combat can be ranked as MICRO on the Richter scale of fears (for example, fear of getting a paper cut, fear of biting your tongue), and the hardest ones to combat can be ranked as CATASTROPHIC (for example, fear of loneliness, fear of not hitting "save" on your manuscript and losing everything you've ever written forever, fear of failure).

Rank your fears using the following scale:

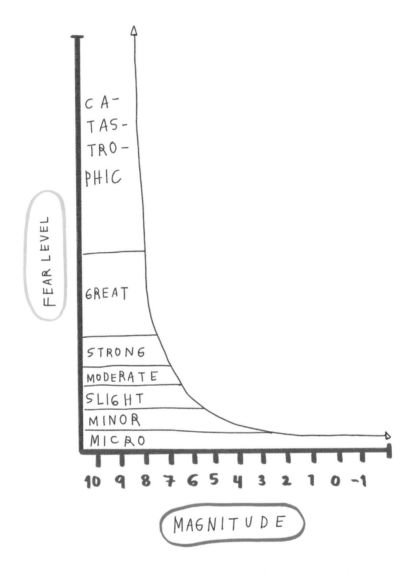

RICHTER SCALE OF FEARS

Ranking your fears will help you begin to understand how they work. Usually, your biggest fear is the one that's been with you the longest. And it is so scary to you that you really don't feel like conquering it—you'd rather not think about it ever again. And I get you. I feel the same way.

Small fears don't have the same size, power, or effect, and they are probably newer to you. They haven't had as much time to grow within your body, and thus, they are easier to conquer, to remove, to root out.

As you read this book, think of conquering your MICRO fears first. Erasing their power will give you a sense of confidence that will be helpful as you move toward addressing those CATASTROPHIC fears. By taking small steps, you'll gain practice, so that when you have to face those catastrophic fears, you'll be stronger.

SUPPORT GROUP

**María
Luque**

AND HAVING TO EXPLORE MUSEUMS WITH ONLY THE TOUR GUIDE'S VOICE.

CHAPTER 1

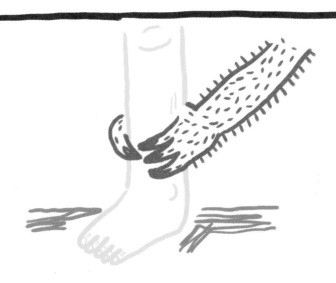

THE ORIGIN OF FEAR

THE SPIDERWEB STRETCHED
TAUT THERE IS THE SPIDERWEB
INSIDE ME. THE BIRDS CALLING
OUT OVERHEAD ARE BIRDS I`VE
FOSTERED IN MY MIND.

— Kafka on the Shore

HARUKI MURAKAMI
Writer
Marathon runner
Hipster idol
Afraid of social interaction

A CLEANING PRODUCT THAT ELIMINATES THE 1% OF BACTERIA THAT ALL OTHER PRODUCTS CAN'T

Fear needs no introduction—we've all felt it. We know how it creeps up, sometimes sneakily and sometimes so abruptly that it makes us run at speeds we didn't know we could reach. We know what it feels like when it takes our heart hostage, when it makes time stop, when it paints the worst-case scenario.

Fear understands us very well.

It knows exactly what triggers it, it knows how to slip under our skin until it lives inside of us—either fleetingly or on a more permanent basis. But how well do we really know it? My theory is that we understand fear very little, or maybe not at all (unless you're Stephen King).

In this book, I hope you will find some things to help you understand fear as well as—or even better than—it understands us.

WHAT IS FEAR?

ACCORDING TO MY MOM

It's when you call me saying you need my help URGENTLY and I yell, "WHAT'S WRONG?" And you respond, "Nothing, Mami, I need help with my book."

ACCORDING TO NINA SIMONE

It is the opposite of freedom.

ACCORDING TO OPRAH

It is only a mask that you have to remove in order to find courage.

ACCORDING TO MY PSYCHIATRIST

Sometimes fear is more biological than it is psychological, and it is caused by alert signals received by the limbic system—specifically, the amygdala, which is located in the temporal lobe.

ACCORDING TO (MY OWN PARAPHRASING OF) WIKIPEDIA*

Fear is an emotion characterized by an intense uncomfortable sensation that arises from the perception of danger, either real or perceived, in the present, the future, or even in the past.

It is a primary emotion derived from a natural aversion to risks or threats, and it manifests itself in many animals, including human beings.

The maximum expression of fear is TERROR. Furthermore, fear is related to ANXIETY.

---

* Let whoever doesn't use Wikipedia as their primary source of information cast the first stone. Besides, to the disappointment of the whole world (and my inner child), Encarta and the Encyclopedia Britannica no longer exist. RIP.

ACCORDING TO FREUD

There are two kinds of fear:

1. REAL FEAR

When the intensity of the fear corresponds to the intensity of the threat (see Figure 1).

2. NEUROTIC FEAR

When the intensity of the fear has absolutely NO relation to the actual degree of danger (see Figure 2).

Fig. 1

Fig. 2

REAL FEAR

NEUROTIC FEAR

OTHER DEFINITIONS GATHERED FROM AN INFORMAL POLL OF FRIENDS AND FAMILY AND SOCIAL MEDIA

Fear is when I make something up and then wind up believing it.

@angelatcomunica

Fear is being alone in a room with a flying cockroach.

My aunt María Eugenia

Fear is wanting something so badly that when you finally get it, you don't think you deserve it.　　　　**@caffetina**

Fear is when my girlfriend tells me we need to talk.　　**@alee_s17**

Fear is when cleaning products say they eliminate 99 percent of bacteria. What about the other 1 percent?　　**Erika Gutiérrez**

Fear is not being able to count on myself when I need to the most.

@samichammas

Fear is when you're driving with the window open and a buzzard gets too close to you, so close that you think it will become your copilot or it will peck at you until you turn into a human with buzzard superpowers (kind of like Spider-Man).　　**@Anamumu**

Sometimes, fear is simply laziness that is allowed to grow and grow and grow.   **@subtleways1**

It's that thing you feel when the scoop of ice cream isn't stuck to the cone firmly enough and you get anxious thinking about whether you should lick it or bite it or just die.   **@danielmoralesa**

Fear is everyone laughing at you after you fall down in public.
                                              The Itsy Bitsy Spider

Write down your own definition of fear—like Mom's, Oprah's, or Nina Simone's—here.

Fear.
Also called "phobia". From the greek
phobos.

A BRIEF ENCYCLOPEDIA
oF FEAR

T o get started on the process of unmasking your fears, it's good to understand how fear works and where it comes from.

HISTORY OF FEAR

Fear is as old as humanity itself. In prehistoric times, people surely weren't afraid of their governments or climate change or sending a screenshot to the wrong person, but they were afraid of lightning storms. Fear (and the way we perceive it) is subject to historical conditions and contexts (the same way we view love). In order to understand fear a little better, let's look at how people have seen it through time.

Aristotle thought that fear was the opposite of confidence and that it could be overcome through virtuous acts (for example: being confident, generous, brave, and kind. Aristotle thought that if you focused on being a good person, then

ARISTOTLE

the right actions to be one would come to you without effort). However, he also thought fear was a sign of a balanced life, and those who didn't manifest it were considered crazy.

COMMON FEARS OF THE MIDDLE AGES

During medieval times, fear wasn't considered a sensation caused by emotional situations or lived experiences, but instead people believed it was a response to an imbalance in "the four corporeal humors."

SCARY NUN

After deciding that fear couldn't be cured through "bloodletting" in order to get rid of an "excess of humors," humanity changed the way it felt about fear.

THE FOUR CORPOREAL HUMORS CHART

HUMOR	TEMPERAMENT	VERB
BLOOD	COURAGEOUS	HELP
YELLOW BILE	CHOLERIC	COMMAND
BLACK BILE	MELANCHOLIC	EVADE
PHLEM	INDIFFERENT	OBTAIN

Look back at this chart when you are in the middle of an existential crisis so you can think things like, "I'm not a coward, I just have an excess of black bile."

COMMON FEARS OF THE EIGHTEENTH CENTURY

FEAR OF
DEATH

FEAR OF
DAMNATION
OF THE SOUL

FEAR OF
WITCHCRAFT

FEAR OF
MILITARY
RAIDS

All the aforementioned fears
have been SPONSORED BY
THE HOLY CATHOLIC CHURCH

COMMON FEARS OF THE NINETEENTH AND TWENTIETH CENTURIES

FEAR OF BEING BURIED ALIVE

FEAR OF INVISIBLE BACTERIA/VIRUSES THAT CAN CAUSE FATAL ILLNESSES

FEAR OF NATURAL DISASTERS

FEAR OF AN ALIEN INVASION

FEAR OF DEGENERATIVE
ILLNESSES LIKE CANCER
OR AIDS

This is still a current fear.
Thanks global leaders who shall
remain unnamed, even though we
all know who you are.

FEAR OF NUCLEAR CONFLICT

NOTE: *We're in the twenty-first century and I'm still afraid of all the things I just named. Especially witchcraft.* ABOVE ALL witchcraft. Is it because I am Latina, and for Latina mothers every bad thing that happens to a human being can be blamed on evil sources? Yes. Do I understand this is mere superstition? Sure. Does this make me fear witchcraft any less? HELL NO. Will I become a victim of this scourge after making that confession? PLEASE, all of you creative folks who are in tune with witchcraft, don't do anything to me. Just in case, I'm also going to invoke Saint Benedict and my beloved Selena as a form of perpetual protection. (If you have the same fears as me or you just broke up with someone who*

Selena

Saint Benedict

---

* By witchcraft, I don't mean lighting candles or doing love spells. I mean dark forces. I mean rituals where there is blood from sacrificed goats mixed with human hair and cemetery soil to set curses upon people.

practices witchcraft and is giving you the evil eye, you may use these drawings to prevent anything bad from EVER happening to you.)

IF YOU HAVE NO IDEA WHO SELENA OR SAINT BENEDICT ARE, WORRY NOT. WRITE OR DRAW THE PEOPLE, SAINTS, PROTECTIVE MANTRAS, AND ANYTHING ELSE THAT WILL BRING TO YOUR LIFE HEAVENLY PROTECTION AGAINST ALL EVIL.

HISTORY OF COWARDS

Despite their apparent bravery, a lot of very brave people either are or were afraid of some pretty bone-chilling things.

NOTE: Use this list when your fear of _____ (write your fear here) makes you feel like a coward and remember: Oprah is afraid of chewing gum. CHEWING GUM!

SIGMUND
FREUD:

Fear of trains

ALFRED
HITCHCOCK:

Fear of eggs

OPRAH
WINFREY:

Fear of chewing gum

NAPOLEON
BONAPARTE:

Fear of cats

CHER

WHOOPI
GOLDBERG

Fear of airplanes

PETER PAN
(AND HALF OF MY
GENERATION):

Fear of growing up

NICOLE
KIDMAN:

Fear of butterflies

JENNIFER
LAWRENCE:

Fear of Zika

A BRIEF HISTORY OF MALE FEARS

Throughout history, fear has been conceived almost exclusively as a female emotion. Women—weak and sensitive—shriek with fear at the sight of any unsuspected danger (like the surprise appearance of a bug in the living room while we're reading, for example). Meanwhile, men—strong, brave, and reckless—seem to be completely unfamiliar with the feeling of terror.

This misconception is clearly a consequence of patriarchy, which labels women as emotional beings devoid of all reason while condemning men to not have any feelings at all, not even fear.

However (bad news, dear rampant patriarchy), men also feel fear (and they cry). *pretends to be shocked* If you don't believe me, ask my cousin José Félix, who screeches uncontrollably every time he sees a mouse. Or my uncle Pepe, who died alone because he was never able to get over his fear of commitment (RIP Tío Pepe).

Here is a brief collection of fears of some men I know, in their own words:

- Getting beaten up if we don't align with stereotypes
- Feeling afraid
- Not performing well in bed
- Falling in love and suffering from heartbreak
- Our real feelings; we're afraid of appearing weak in front of others
- Zombies

- Not knowing how to love someone more than I love myself
- Being very broken, and of how that could affect my emotions, relationships, and such
- Rejection
- Loving too much
- A *Black Mirror*–type society
- Loneliness; one day realizing I've grown old and am still alone

If you are a man, this might sound redundant, but know that it's okay to have fears. Write your own and explore them with curiosity and gentleness. If you are not a man, ask the men around you about their fears. It seems like a simple conversation, but it is a powerful exercise for creating space for everyone to relate with fear in a healthier way *and* it's also a powerful and personal way to fight THE PATRIARCHY.

SUPPORT GROUP

Alejandro Gómez-Dugand

Breathe. Breathe in with the top part of your chest.
Breathe quickly.
Inhale.
Exhale.
Breathe even if you feel like an elephant is sitting on your chest.

They tell you it's okay, that everything is going to be okay. But even so, people continue to file into an auditorium just a few feet away from you. People who are there to see you on stage and whom you will have to address. You have to do it well. They paid to be in this auditorium and you have to follow through. A few bucks are enough to buy your calm, your ability to speak coherently.

They tell you it's okay, that it's all going to be okay. But it's useless, so put your hands in your pockets so nobody can see how much they're shaking.

That fear, the fear they call stage fright, is very similar to the fear of dying. It's an evolutionary lag, it's my primitive self preparing for fight or flight. Muscles tense, ready to throw a rock or take off. Pupils dilated, the size of plates, my sight focused on the horizon where I'll finally be able to leave the sabertooth that's threatening to devour me behind. Everything in front of me—the paper I'm supposed to read from on stage, for example—is a blurry smudge.

They tell me it's okay, that I'm going to be okay. And yet I still run to the bathroom. I have read, more than enough times, that this isn't anything but a biological misunderstanding. I'm about to step onto a stage where nothing seriously bad can happen to me, but my body is convinced I'm being preyed upon by a wild creature. So, I try to trick it, make it see reason.

I breathe. I breathe, trying to do it through my nose. I inhale and exhale. I move my body into the Wonder Woman pose—legs slightly apart and hands on my hips—to tell my body we're in control, that everything's okay. My body responds with nausea.

And then I have to go out. I have to walk into the auditorium filled with sabertooths. I say hi. I say I'm happy to be here.

Happy, I say.

The fear folds onto itself,
folds onto itself,
folds onto itself.

Until finally, it's small enough that I could fit it into my pocket.

THE PHYSICAL AND EMOTIONAL ANATOMY OF FEAR

Fear works on two fronts: emotional and physical. This is how intense terror takes hold of your body.

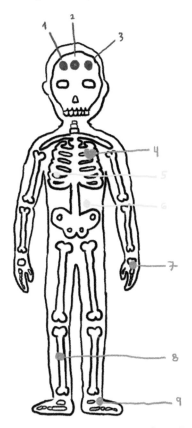

SOMEONE WHO IS SCARED TO
DEATH ON THE INSIDE

1. The brain perceives a threat and sends out signals, entering a state of alertness. Fear is a VERY uncomfortable physical sensation, but at the same time it can give us superpowers—literally. The adrenaline that courses through our veins when we're scared to death can be enough to lift a car or run like the Flash.

2. Any memories related to that fear are activated.

3. On a psycho-emotional level, an internal monologue that goes more or less like this unfolds: "Why did I agree to give this lecture? I am going to faint. My mind is going to go blank. My heart is about to jump out of my chest. My hands are going to sweat so much I get dehydrated. I'm going to die. I swear on my love for my mother that I'm never going to do this again. I need to escape."

4. The heart is not bursting out of the chest quite yet, but it's close. Heartrate increases due to adrenaline and cortisone.

5. The breathing quickens and lung capacity increases (paradoxically).

6. The stomach collapses (it doesn't really, but that's what it feels like). Extreme fear can lead to stomach discomfort, nausea, or even vomiting.

7. Extensive sweating and shaking begin, especially in the hands.

8. The brain pumps lots of blood to the legs in case we need to run for our lives. At the same time, some other form of wizardry occurs and makes the legs start to feel like jelly.

9. We are ready to fight, flight, or freeze—in mind, body, and spirit.

NOTE: The aforementioned reactions are triggered in the same way whether we are confronted with the possibility of physical or emotional danger. This is why getting our hearts broken can be just as scary, or even scarier, than encountering a killer shark in open sea.

WHERE FEARS ARE BORN

We all experience fear in our bodies in more or less the same way. However, the emotional path terror takes and its psychological consequences vary from person to person.

Most of our fears have their origin in our memories or in things we can't control, or they are a mystery to us.

MEMORIES

THE ENEMY

EXAMPLE:

When my favorite cousin was six years old, my aunt María Eugenia's French poodle bit him. To this day, he is terrified of dogs.*

---

* I was there at the moment, but I didn't come to the rescue because I was too busy eating the French poodle's food (his name was Benji, I think) because it smelled delicious.

NOTE: Dog food does NOT taste how it smells.

THINGS WE CAN'T CONTROL

THE OCEAN

WHETHER OR NOT
SOMEONE LOVES US

HURRICANES
(EMOTIONAL OR
METEOROLOGICAL, OR
BOTH)

STRANGE NEW VIRUSES THAT
THREATEN TO TURN THE WORLD
INTO THAT GWYNETH PALTROW MOVIE

WHETHER THINGS WILL
WORK THE WAY WE
WANT THEM TO

CURRENT
WORLD
POLITICS

Almost all of our fears are preemptive reactions to something terrible happening based on negative experiences we've had in the past or on our lack of ability to control a situation. Our fears exist more in our heads than they do outside of them. The really scary thing is not a venomous snake bite that could end your life in half a minute, an earthquake, an alien invasion, or the end of the world. The really scary thing is the way fear paralyzes us, annihilates us, strips us of all reason. The scary thing is the list of things we stop doing when we're afraid, the silences we nurture, the shortcuts we start to take to avoid facing anything, anyone, even our own selves. The scary thing is when fear turns into an obstacle, a trap, an excuse. When we become emotional hypochondriacs, always ready to look for a diagnosis that can confirm our suspicions and validate our insecurities and paranoias.

MYSTERIES OF THE HUMAN MIND

Better known as irrational fears or phobias.

AILUROPHOBIA
Fear of cats

EMOTIONAL ARCHEOLOGY

Time to put your memory to work. The good thing about this exercise is that it's a good mental workout. The bad thing is that you will have to perform a historical reconstruction of your emotional past. Digging into your memories will help you trace where or how your deepest fears first appeared in your life. Once you can trace a moment (you don't have to be exact, don't worry), try to describe what was happening at that specific time in your life. Do you remember how you were feeling? Where were you? Was your family with you? Answering these questions will help you better understand your personal terrors, better equipping you to conquer them.

WRITE OR DRAW THE MEMORIES THAT CREATED YOUR FEARS HERE:

THE END (for now)

SUPPORT GROUP

**Power
Paola**

CHAPTER 2

MONSTERS UNDER THE BED AND OTHER FAMILIAR FEARS

MONSTERS ARE REAL, AND GHOSTS
ARE REAL, TOO. THEY LIVE INSIDE
US, AND SOMETIMES, THEY WIN.

— Introduction to *The Shining*

STEPHEN KING
Author
Supreme pontiff of terror on earth
Afraid of memory loss and/or going mad

Our first encounter with fear happens during our childhood, when we constantly worry about being snatched by the boogeyman or when we have to run from an imminent goose attack.*

But our fears evolve with us. Some settle into us forever, others change their appearance, and others grow with the passing of time. Truly understanding the monsters that still live and that used to live under our beds is essential to unmasking them, conquering them, and taking power from them.

---

* If you were never chased by a goose or by another bird that looks harmless but is actually extremely violent, you should feel extremely lucky and replace this fear with one you actually felt.

FEARS FROM THE
PAST

FEAR OF TREES GROWING
INSIDE OF US AFTER
SWALLOWING A SEED

MOM?

FEAR OF BEING LEFT
BEHIND AT THE GROCERY
STORE

FEAR OF BURGLARS
BREAKING INTO THE
HOUSE

BUS

FEAR OF LOSING AN
ARM AFTER STICKING
IT OUT OF A CAR/ BUS
WINDOW

FEAR OF SHARKS
(EVEN IN POOLS)

FEAR OF A BUG CRAWLING
INTO YOUR MOUTH AFTER
FALLING ASLEEP WITH IT OPEN

I regret to inform you that your daughter's intestines are stuck together.

FEAR OF YOUR INTESTINES
STICKING TOGETHER AFTER
SWALLOWING A PIECE OF GUM

Sup! I appear AND talk to people. JUST LIKE GHOSTS. Yay!

FEAR OF A MIRACULOUS
APPARITION OF THE VIRGIN
MARY

PRESENT FEARS

FEAR OF CREDIT CARDS

FEAR OF ROMANTIC BREAKUPS

LIST OF NEW YEAR'S RESOLUTIONS:

- TO UNDERSTAND MY SELF-WORTH IS *not* DERIVED FROM MY PRODUCTIVITY.
- TO IMPROVE MY HEALTH.
- TO NEVER HAVE MY HEART BROKEN EVER AGAIN.

FEAR OF LOSING OUR
PARENTS / FRIENDS /
FAMILY MEMBERS

FEAR OF THE FUTURE

FEAR OF COMMITMENT

FEAR OF FAILURE

BIRD'S-EYE VIEW

FEAR OF SOLITUDE

FEAR OF REJECTION

YOUR OWN FEARS OF THE PAST

You know what to do. WRITE OR DRAW YOUR PAST FEARS HERE:

_____

_____

_____

_____

_____

_____

_____

_____

_____

_____

YOUR OWN PRESENT
FEARS

Here, too.

_____

_____

_____

_____

_____

_____

_____

_____

_____

_____

_____

SUPPORT GROUP

ALEJANDRA ALGORTA

The first autonomous decision I ever made in my life was that I had to be able to see light coming through the curtains in my bedroom. I say it's the first one because I don't remember much else from that time period. My brother would exile me from our room using independence as his excuse, Mom would show me samples of different blues and violets to paint the walls, and the only thing I asked of those fourteen square meters was that they weren't dark.

That decision, like many others that I would make throughout the years, was not good for me. Perhaps if the tree branches projected onto the curtains didn't look so much like the claws of an enemy, or if the warm light of the Bogotá streets could tame the cold, perhaps if I wasn't always the last one to fall asleep, I wouldn't have felt so much fear.

I remember shaking. I remember spending what I thought were hours trying to get to my parents' bed without waking them up. Leaning weightlessly against my mom's side of the bed, pressing my back against hers and feeling the warmth of a person who's alive, of a person who breathes, of a person who sleeps. I remember the relief with which I would finally fall asleep at her side.

It made no difference that the shadows of the trees at my window were projected by a light. To me, darkness—even at night nowadays—has always represented a land of possibilities. The possibility that everyone I love will fall asleep and never wake up again. The possibility that the branches on the trees will grab me with their bony arms and wrap around me until I suffocate. The possibility of everything around me disappearing forever as soon as I close my eyes. The possibility of a hairy caterpillar climbing into my mouth if I sleep with it open. The possibility that, when I approach her bed, my mother's chest won't move, won't breathe. Nothing could guarantee that my family, horizontal and unconscious on the other side of the violet-colored walls, was still alive.

So far the sun has always risen, and darkness has brought with it possibilities that aren't so terrible. The possibility of getting close to another body and noticing it only at the brush of an eyelash, the possibility of perceiving through touch and skin rather than sight. And finally, the possibility of light. And the knowledge that not existing must feel very similar to closing your eyes and not being able to see inside, because it's dark.

TYPES OF FEARS
(AND HOW TO READ THEM)

We already know that our fears live inside us, and we already know what they are. Now we have to focus on understanding what they mean.

In the following pages, you'll find six types of basic fears all human beings share, according to Karl Albrecht (who has devoted his life to understanding what fear does to us and how it works). The first five correspond to instinctual fears that all human beings feel. The sixth one was invented by me. And the internet. Mostly the internet. These types of fear both contain and explain the root of AL-MOST ALL of our fears. A fear can come from any category or from a combination of two or more.

Always keep in mind that a fear is not just a fear. Behind our fears lie painful things, on one hand, and powerful things, on the other. Understanding our fears will always be a source of wisdom and power.

1. NO THANKS, I'D RATHER LIVE

FEAR OF EXTINCTION

Fear of stopping, dying, ceasing to exist. This fear arises the exact moment we realize we're alive and stays with us until the day we die. The thought of dying produces anxiety in all human beings, even in those who say "Death? Nah, I'm not scared of that."

HOW TO IDENTIFY IT

This fear presents itself with the following disguises:

FEAR OF HEIGHTS

Public Restroom

└→ person performing
a balancing act to flush
a public toilet and save
themselves from Ebola.

FEAR OF GERMS/
BACTERIA/ILLNESSES

Stop pretending that being
in a gigantic metallic thing
that flies is natural. This
is NOT natural.

FEAR OF AIRPLANES

2. CONSIDER HAN SOLO GETTING FROZEN IN CARBONITE

FEAR OF LOSING AUTONOMY

Fear of being trapped, locked in, or wrapped up (like a mummy). Fear of being paralyzed, suffocated, drowned. Of being controlled by external circumstances, people, surroundings, or illnesses from which we cannot escape.

HOW TO IDENTIFY IT

OBVIOUS INTERPRETATION

Claustrophobia
Fear of growing old and wearing diapers again
Fear of elevators

NOT-SO-OBVIOUS INTERPRETATION

Fear of losing economic security
Fear of unfair/mediocre bosses who make us feel helpless

WINNING INTERPRETATION

Fear of commitment
Fear of intimacy

3. ARMS OUT

FEAR OF MUTILATION

Fear of our bodily integrity being threatened in any way, meaning fear of losing an arm, an organ, or one of our natural bodily functions. Fear of being unable to use a leg, of not feeling one of our hands, of losing one or more fingers.

These are some of the ways the fear of mutilation manifests itself.

HOW TO IDENTIFY IT

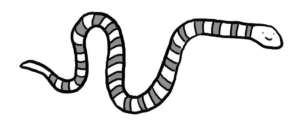

FEAR OF SNAKES

FEAR OF BATS

FEAR OF NEEDLES

FEAR OF BUGS

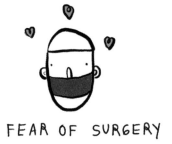

FEAR OF SURGERY

FEAR OF SPIDERS

4. THE ORIGINAL FEAR

FEAR OF SEPARATION

Here's the thing: we are in our birth mother's womb and we are happy. Then we're born and, subconsciously, we spend our entire life trying to find wombs outside the womb (don't look at me, this is coming from Freud and from my obsession with beds and blankets). I call this the Original Fear because it stems from the separation from our mothers after birth.

HOW TO IDENTIFY IT

This is the fear of rejection, of abandonment, of the rupture of emotional links. It's the fear of not being loved, of being left on read, of being FOREVER ALONE.*

---

* BACK OFF, SATAN

JEALOUSY (YES, JEALOUSY IS FEAR)

FEAR OF GHOSTING

FEAR OF ABANDONMENT

FEAR OF EMOTIONAL
"FAILURE"

5. IT'S NOT ME, IT'S YOU

FEAR OF EGO DEATH

This type of fear encompasses everything that could put the integrity of the self at risk, shatter the construction of our identity, erase that little something we feel makes us who we are, and threaten our feeling that we are worthy and capable of giving and receiving love, respect, and admiration.

HOW TO IDENTIFY IT

This is the fear of being humiliated, and the fear of embarrassment or profound disapproval from our own selves or at the hands of others.

I was fired, but I'm taking the stapler because that's what they do in the movies

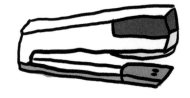

FEAR OF LOSING YOUR JOB

FEAR OF PUBLIC SPEAKING

FEAR OF BULLYING/
HARASSMENT

FEAR OF FAILURE

6. IF I DIE, DELETE MY SCREENSHOTS

FEARS OF THE NEW MILLENNIUM

These fears don't need an explanation—they hound us every three minutes (thanks to social media and smartphones) and, sometimes, they don't even leave us alone while we sleep.

You can read them however you please.

FEAR OF THE CAMERA ON YOUR PHONE OR COMPUTER BEING USED AS A TOOL FOR ESPIONAGE

NOTIFICATION:

The girl you like has just taken a screenshot of your conversation, which is now being analyzed by all of her friends.

FEAR OF YOUR PHONE
SENDING NOTIFICATIONS
EVERY TIME YOU SCREENSHOT
A TEXT

FEAR OF ACCIDENTALLY
LIKING A PHOTO DURING AN
ONLINE STALKING SESSION,
USUALLY ONE POSTED
593 DAYS AGO

WRITE OR DRAW SOME OF YOUR GREATEST FEARS OF THE
NEW MILLENNIUM HERE:

_____

_____

_____

_____

_____

_____

_____

_____

_____

_____

_____

_____

LIVING THROUGH YOUR FEARS

At this point, you're probably thinking that the title of this book should actually be *A Compilation of Fears*.

But it's also about how to live through them. And it's not as difficult as you might think.

The reason for this is simple: there are only two ways to get rid of fear. The first is through gaining a profound understanding of it and the second is by looking it right in the eyes.

EXERCISE

On the following page, you must:

- Pretend as though you're drinking some tea/a cup of coffee/whatever you want with your fears.
- Unleash the gossipiest version of yourself to get A LOT of information out of them.
- Ask your own fear questions such as: What triggers you? How do you feel once you are triggered? What calms you? What is the best-case scenario? What is the worst-case scenario? How does it feel when fear is at its maximum? How does it feel when such fear is overcome?
- Draw or write the information you learn.*

Based on the information you obtain, try to sort your fears into the aforementioned categories. This will help you unveil the REAL fear behind your fears. (Remember: fear is a tricky dude.)

For example:

I had an earnest one-on-one talk with my fear of flying. I learned that *surprise* it is triggered by turbulence, mild turbulence to be specific. Once the ride gets bumpy my fear goes crazy. I start fantasizing about the plane falling out of the sky even though I've read a thousand times that that is literally impossible (turbulence doesn't take planes down) and that it's more probable that I'll die slipping on a banana than in a plane crash. When the turbulence is light, my heart skips a beat and my hands get sweaty, but when it gets rough,

---

* Fear is supremely self-centered. Self-centered and catastrophic. Self-centered and catastrophic and exaggerated. Try not to give it that much of your attention but listen to it VERY carefully. Don't fight against it—rather, try to make it believe it's right, but on the inside, know that it's NOT.

I inhabit an awful liminal space where I feel at the verge of a panic attack all the time and that puts me in awful psychological pain.

Learning this helped me understand that my fear of flying is also A FEAR OF EXTINCTION (I fear I am going to die), but mostly A FEAR OF LOSING AUTONOMY (what I fear the most is being controlled by my anxiety to an extent that I can do nothing about it and, paradoxically, I lose it).

EXERCISE

SUPPORT GROUP

Herikita

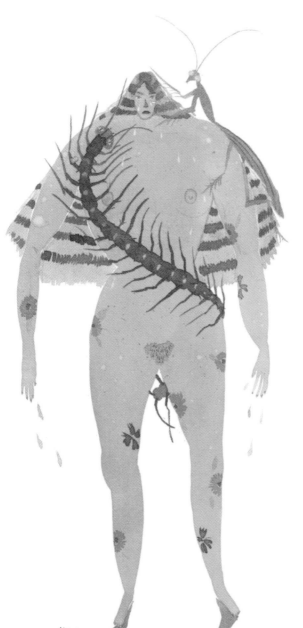

MY WORST FEAR IS ALL OF MY FEARS TOGETHER

HEAIKITA 2017

CHAPTER 3

PRISON OF FEAR

FEAR AS A PRISON

FEAR CAN CAUSE BLINDNESS, SAID THE
GIRL WITH DARK GLASSES, NEVER A
TRUER WORD, THAT COULD NOT BE TRUER,
WE WERE ALREADY BLIND THE MOMENT
WE TURNED BLIND, FEAR STRUCK US
BLIND, FEAR WILL KEEP US BLIND.

— *Blindness*

JOSÉ SARAMAGO
Writer
Established atheist
Afraid of being forgotten

ear can be a natural (and healthy) response to many threats. But it can also be a prison. A prison of terror that we build with care to keep from changing our habits, chasing our dreams, taking a leap into the unknown. Fear is often one of the most effective methods of self-sabotage, the most successful way to ensure we always stay within comfort zones disguised as well-being (when, in reality, they always harm us in the end).

This is the kind of fear that paralyzes us, binds us, whispers in our ear and tells us it has lots of power, that it's too large, that we can't overcome it.

LIES.

LIST OF THINGS
I HAVEN'T DONE
BECAUSE OF FEAR

1. Go to an important literary festival as an invited panelist (fear of airplanes)

2. Visit beautiful landmarks in Colombia, spend weekends at friends' country houses, go on a road trip from Cali to Bogotá (fear of getting dizzy in a car)

3. Talk about my fears (fear of my fears coming true as soon as I say them out loud)

4. Tell P. what I really feel about his neglect (fear of confrontation)

5. Be honest with B. with regards to how her actions hurt me (fear of vulnerability; fear of being ridiculed)

6. Cross the Brooklyn Bridge (fear of heights; fear of crossing the street)

7. Eat things like oysters, brains, or any kind of tartare (fear of vomiting)

LIST OF THINGS
YOU HAVEN'T DONE
BECAUSE OF FEAR

1. _____

2. _____

3. _____

4. _____

5. _____

SUPPORT GROUP

GLORIA SUSANA ESQUIVEL

I know exactly what I would ask the genie from Aladdin's lamp if it appeared in front of me. Unfortunately, you wouldn't find the sovereignty of human dignity and social justice on my list, or unlimited access to mental health professionals for world leaders. You also wouldn't find a house filled with corgi puppies to brighten my days or the complete eradication of the cellulitis that has been with me since I was twelve years old. My only wish for the genie would be much simpler: to become the kind of person who, upon reclining on the headrest of an airplane seat, can fall asleep.

A list of things I haven't done because of my fear of airplanes: attend the poetry festival in Medellin, participate in an exchange semester in Mexico, go on vacation to paradisiac islands with my friends, explore Australia.

A list of things I've done to stop being afraid of airplanes: psychological treatment since I was twenty years old, Reiki, hypnosis, psychoanalysis, overdosing on Dramamine, overdosing on whisky, meditation.

A list of things that have effectively cured my fear of airplanes: none of the above.

This is a fear that has grown with me. These days I no longer avoid airplanes; I force myself to take them despite the psychologic discomfort they cause me. There are moments when I genuinely relax and enjoy the flight, just like the crew instructs you before take-off, and I marvel at the miracle of aviation. But there are others when the slightest bit of turbulence sends me into a state of alertness that makes my hands sweat uncontrollably and leaves me short of breath. There are moments when I'm terrified of taking off and others when I imagine the airplane is a giant bird who swallowed me whole and is flying away with me. On occasions, I've greatly enjoyed landing and seeing distinct aerial views of each city—Mexico City like a concrete wave breaking in the middle of the desert, Bogotá emerging amid a green savanna that resembles a patched quilt—but I've also felt that those moments of descent are complete agony. I used to be incapable of focusing on movies; now I'm only able to travel with relative calm if I'm equipped with a good dose of chick flicks.

I feel like my fear would find relief if I were able to fall into a deep sleep immediately upon getting on an airplane. But that is something that has never, never ever happened.

FEAR AS
SELF-SABOTAGE

The vicious cycle of the prison of terror is like the snake that eats its tail. Fear feeds on fear. That is why it is so easy to get trapped in it. The good news: it's also easy to get out. Fear is a great illusionist, but as with most illusions, once you know how the trick works, its magic is forever put to an end.

Fear of not fulfilling
a dream / Fear of failure

PERPETUATES THE

LEADS TO

Self-sabotage
· Excuses
· procrastination
· Too many hours spent
stalking Harry styles or
whomever
· Harmful actions

Self-invalidation
Guilt
Low self-esteem

RESULTS IN

MY SELF-SABOTAGING THOUGHT PROCESS

FEAR

Fear of nobody wanting to read this book

AUGMENTED BY AN AVERAGE OF 150 HOURS OF OVERTHINKING PER WEEK ⟶

REAL MEANING

Fear of Failure

Fear is not as Funny as heartbreak, the subject of my last book. Nobody wants to read about Fear.

FALSE BELIEF (IF A, THEN B)

If I write a book about Fear, nobody will want to read it.

REINFORCED BY

Selling books is basically a miracle.

UNCERTAINTY /
LACK OF CONTROL

Is this book a good
idea? What if only my
mom buys it?

↓

HOPING THAT
"IF A, THEN B"
WON'T COME TRUE

Books that don't sell
are disposed of like trash.
I don't want this book
to get destroyed.

↓ ↓ ↓ ↓

BELIEF THAT IF I DO
C, THEN A → B WON'T
BE POSSIBLE

If I don't write a scary
book about fear, then
nothing bad can happen

ACTION

SAFE OPTION:
I don't write the book.

LEAP OF FAITH:
I write it.

↑

GROUP CHAT
INTERVENTION
BY MY FRIENDS

"Girl, stop

overthinking and

• write. Bye."

↑

HOW YOUR FEAR WORKS

Chart the thought process of one of your own fears in order to understand how your prison of fear operates. What is your self-sabotaging process? What is your safe option? What is your leap of faith? If you're up for it, take a picture of the results and upload it to Instagram so we can beat our fears together.

FEAR

AUGMENTED BY
AN AVERAGE OF ⟶
150 HOURS OF
OVERTHINKING
PER WEEK

REAL MEANING

FALSE BELIEF
(IF A, THEN B) ⟶ REINFORCED BY

UNCERTAINTY /
LACK OF CONTROL

ACTION

HOPING THAT
"IF A, THEN B"
WON'T COME TRUE

GROUP CHAT
INTERVENTION
BY MY FRIENDS

BELIEF THAT IF I DO
C, THEN A → B WON'T
BE POSSIBLE

WAYS OF BREAKING OUT OF THE VICIOUS CYCLE OF TERROR

Time to stop feeding fear with more fear. Let's feed it with bravery instead. Or just plain reasoning. Or something else that is positive and nurturing. Just DON'T FEED IT WITH MORE FEAR. Thank you. Bye.

ONE

Focus on the fear. Understand where it came from. What is the thought process that led to it? Know that if something went wrong once, it doesn't always have to be that way.

TWO

Understand that failure is necessary for success. Yes, leaps of faith (in love, at work, during major life changes) are scary. But if something doesn't work out it WON'T be the end of the world. Quite the contrary, it will help you grow and do things better next time.

THREE

Think of your entire life as trial and error. This may sound reductionist or cruel in some cases—when it comes to love, for example—but that's just how it is. If a relationship (or an attempt at one) didn't work out, please DON'T think that things will always be this way. (This also applies to bumpy airplane flights, presidents that should never have been elected, rejected projects, that time when you finally decided to be emotionally open and it didn't work out.)

It's painful, but look back at all the things you learned, and instead of being paralyzed by fear, dare to go for it again and use the information you've acquired instead of looking for excuses to stay in a safe place.

ANTI-FEAR KIT

Take this kit with you at all times (or at the very least, don't ever forget about it). It helps soothe fears, ease nightmares, and remind you that your dreams are bigger than your fears.

PLAYLIST TO HELP YOU DO ALL THE THINGS YOU'RE SCARED OF DOING

Goodbye, fear. Hello, courage. Use this playlist every time you feel like fear is taking you over and tell it: "Don't bother getting up—you're not coming with me."

- "Burn" by Ellie Goulding
- "Bulletproof" by La Roux
- "Run the World (Girls)" by Beyoncé
- "The Greatest" by Sia featuring Kendrick Lamar
- "I Feel It All" by Feist
- "It's My Life" by No Doubt
- "I Wanna Get Better" by Bleachers
- "Unstoppable" by Sia
- "Feel Good Inc." by Gorillaz
- "The Zephyr Song" by Red Hot Chili Peppers
- "I Want to Break Free" by Queen
- "Safe and Sound" by Capital Cities
- "Starboy" by The Weeknd featuring Daft Punk
- "Masseducation" by St. Vincent
- "Fast Slow Disco" by St. Vincent

Write your personal playlist here:

> _____

> _____

> _____

> _____

> _____

> _____

> _____

> _____

> _____

> _____

> _____

LIST OF MOVIES THAT WILL MAKE YOU SAY "IF X COULD DO IT, I CAN DO IT, TOO"

SPIRITED AWAY

TO KILL A MOCKINGBIRD

WHAT WE DO IN THE SHADOWS

NEVER BEEN KISSED

LOLA VERSUS

FRANCES HA

BRAVE

GRAVITY

MERMAIDS

THE PURSUIT OF
HAPPYNESS

ARRIVAL

RISE OF THE
GUARDIANS

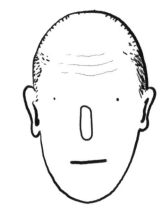

BEING JOHN MALKOVICH

LIST OF BOOKS THAT WILL INSPIRE YOU TO BE FEARLESS

> Where the Wild Things Are by Maurice Sendak
> Letting Go of Gravity by Meg Leder
> Fun Home by Alison Bechdel
> In the Dream House by Carmen Maria Machado
> The Outsiders by S. E. Hinton
> Fiebre Tropical by Juliana Delgado Lopera
> A Manual For Cleaning Women by Lucia Berlin
> Wild by Cheryl Strayed
> Lost Children Archive by Valeria Luiselli
> The House on Mango Street by Sandra Cisneros
> A Confederacy of Dunces by John Kennedy Toole

INSTRUCTIONS

Cut out this poster. Stick it on the door of your room/office/bath-room.

MY DREAMS
ARE BIGGER
THAN MY
F·E·A·R·S

SUPPORT GROUP

Milena Hachim

FEAR OF SPEAKING IN PUBLIC OR WITH PEOPLE I DON'T KNOW

CHAPTER 4

WHEN FEAR SPIRALS OUT OF CONTROL

IT SEEMS TO ME THAT WE NEVER SERIOUSLY
INQUIRED WHY THE NERVOUS SUFFERED SO MUCH
MORE AND SO MUCH MORE INTENSELY UNDER THE CONDITION
[OF FEAR]. PERHAPS IT WAS THOUGHT A MATTER OF
COURSE; IT IS USUAL TO CONFUSE THE WORDS "NERVOUS"
AND "ANXIOUS" AS THOUGH THEY MEANT THE SAME
THING. THAT IS UNJUSTIFIABLE; THERE ARE
ANXIOUS PEOPLE WHO ARE NOT NERVOUS, AND
NERVOUS PEOPLE WHO SUFFER FROM MANY
SYMPTOMS, BUT NOT FROM THE TENDENCY
TO ANXIETY.
— A General Introduction to Psychoanalysis

SIGMUND FREUD
Father of psychoanalysis
Antique collector
Afraid of firearms

I NEVER KNOW IF WHAT I'M FEELING IS HUNGER, A MIGRAINE, DIZZINESS, OR AN ANXIETY ATTACK.

Recently, anxiety has enjoyed more time in the spotlight. It shows up in memes, in articles, on the news. It shows up in pictures, on Instagram, in press releases by millennial artists. The bad thing about this is that now it's easy to confuse any kind of nervousness with an anxiety disorder. The good thing about this is that the topic is gaining visibility, it's being given the importance it deserves, and mental health is finally being discussed.

Before we go too far, given that an anxiety disorder can be a very serious issue, consider the following:

- It is best to consult with a therapist before mistaking a very spooky scare with panic and anxiety attacks.
- This chapter is not a replacement for adequate anxiety treatment in the hands of a therapist.
- The words written here are meant to make you laugh, to console you, to let you know that you're not alone. PLEASE don't take them as a diagnostic tool (it's tempting, I know, but that's what psychiatrists are for).
- You are you and I am me and anxiety is different for every person. Each person deals with this issue as best they can, or however their trusted specialist recommends.

WHAT IS THE DIFFERENCE BETWEEN EVERYDAY FEAR AND AN ANXIETY DISORDER?

Anxiety disorders are usually characterized by fear that:

Is overwhelming and impossible to manage. Seriously considering getting a puppet made with your face so it can take your place in situations that are apparently normal for other human beings (social/work gatherings, project presentations, speaking in public) but that for us who suffer from anxiety feel like HORRIBLE torture.

Is chronic. A near constant desire to have the ability to reset your life and your mind the way you can reset a cell phone, so you could put an end to the overthinking, the racing heartbeat, the sweating, or the feeling of anguish that seems to appear out of nowhere.

Involves catastrophic thinking. "WHAT IF I SOMEDAY BUY A HOUSE AND DON'T INSURE IT AND THEN IT CATCHES FIRE AND I'M LEFT WITH NOTHING? AND THAT'S BEING OPTIMISTIC, ASSUMING THAT I'LL ONE DAY BE ABLE TO BUY A HOUSE. WHAT IF I FAIL AND DO NOTHING WITH MY LIFE AND DIE ALONE AND FORGOTTEN? OR WHAT IF ONE DAY I GET PREGNANT AND GET ONE OF THOSE STRANGE MEDICAL

Hello, I'M AMALIA'S ANXIETY.
TODAY WE SPENT 5 HOURS
READING ABOUT RARE
ILLNESSES WE'RE NOW SURE
WE HAVE, ALSO WE'RE NOT
GOING TO GET ANY SLEEP
TONIGHT THINKING ABOUT

THAT EMBARRASSING THING
THAT HAPPENED 12 YEARS
AGO. YAY!

CONDITIONS THAT THEY SHOW ON DISCOVERY HOME AND HEALTH?" And so forth. Forever and ever. The end.

Interferes with everyday life functions. Taking more than two days (it could be two years) to respond to text messages or emails because "I CAN'T DO EVERYTHING IN LIFE. THIS PLUS THE OTHER TWO THINGS I NEED TO DO DURING THE DAY ARE TOO MUCH FOR ME, AND BESIDES, WHAT AM I GOING TO SAY? HOW DO I BEGIN THIS EMAIL? I SHOULD RESPOND TOMORROW. IT'S BEEN THREE MONTHS AND I STILL HAVEN'T RESPONDED. NOW WHAT AM I SUPPOSED TO SAY? WOULD THEY BELIEVE ME IF I PRETEND MY CAT BIT BOTH MY HANDS OFF?"

TYPES OF ANXIETY DISORDERS

According to experts, anxiety can appear as one of five different types.*

1. OBSESSIVE-COMPULSIVE DISORDER (OCD)

This disorder is particularly difficult to define, so I will give you the example of my friend Isabel.** Isabel says that she is usually haunted by obsessive thoughts that feel like intruders in her head. These obsessive thoughts constantly tell her that it's very likely that, at any moment, one of her family members will die suddenly. But if she carries out a compulsive ritual—which consists of touching different objects in her house in a specific order more than seven times, and which has to be completely restarted if interrupted—she feels

---

* And by experts, I mean the men and women from the American Psychiatric Association who write the *Diagnostic and Statistical Manual of Mental Disorders*, or as I like to call it *The Anxiety Bible* (even though if you are a really anxious person, which you probably are because you are reading this book, I discourage you from ever accessing it, as it may lead you to believe you are currently going through most of the psychiatric problems listed within the pages, or at least that was my experience). Many of the concepts mentioned in this book are written about there, but at more length and explained more clearly (or less clearly, depending on how you look at it. . . . .).

** Isabel isn't really my friend. Or she is. She's my imaginary friend. She's my friend who doesn't know she's my friend yet. In any event, Isabel is a girl from the Discovery Home and Health show whose case moved me to my core.

like she has done everything in her power to keep her family safe. This process takes Isabel almost three and a half hours, and she recognizes that it is irrational and disproportionate.

Thus, OCD consists of:

- Obsessions: constant thoughts, images, ideas, or impulses that produce anxiety and feel intrusive.
- Compulsions: mental behaviors or actions that are meant to neutralize the obsession, ease and contain the anxiety, or prevent a negative event.

TABLE OF OBSESSIONS AND COMPULSIONS

O: Contracting an illness from shaking someone's hand.

C: Washing your hands until you bleed.

O: Wondering whether you left the stove on.

C: Checking the stove every five minutes, coming back from work to check the stove, thinking of nothing else because you're worried about the damned stove.

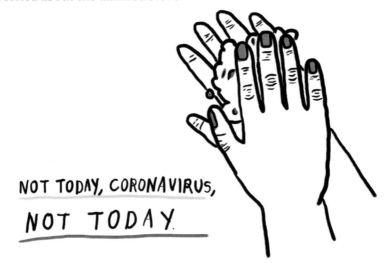

NOT TODAY, CORONAVIRUS, NOT TODAY.

2. POST-TRAUMATIC STRESS DISORDER (PTSD)

PTSD is defined as a series of symptoms that appear after exposure to a traumatic event during which the individual is usually confronted by a danger (for example, being a victim of a crime, abuse, or accident) that puts their own life, their physical integrity, or someone else's life at risk. Said symptoms include intense nightmares, fear, despair, persistent flashbacks of the traumatic event, and avoidance of trauma-related stimuli.

3. SOCIAL ANXIETY DISORDER (SOCIAL PHOBIA)

Social anxiety disorder is a persistent and intense fear of situations that require social exposure or interaction for fear that they can become embarrassing. It's not about your legs shaking before you introduce yourself to a room full of strangers or being scared of talking to people at a party where you only know the host who just decided to go out and buy more drinks, disappearing for an hour and leaving you without any company. Rather, it's an intense panic that can lead you to avoid simple actions like eating, writing, or speaking in public for fear that you will be ridiculed or that people will think you seem nervous, shaky, anxious, weak, foolish, or "crazy." It tends to be accompanied by panic attacks and reddening of the face (among many other things).

NOTE: *Social anxiety disorder is a type of phobia. A phobia is an intense, irrational, and disproportionate fear of a situation, person, or object. What follows is a collection of exceptional phobics who prove that we are not alone, even in our most particular fears.*

Kendall Jenner
_____

TRYPOPHOBIA
(Fear of irregular patterns,
or clusters of small holes)

Anthony Bourdain
_____

COULROPHOBIA
(Fear of clowns)

Johnny Cash
_____

OPHIDIOPHOBIA
(Fear of snakes)

Lena Dunham

SOMNIPHOBIA
(Fear of going to sleep)

Steve Jobs

KOUMPOUNOPHOBIA
(Fear of buttons, hence
all those turtlenecks)

Richard Wagner

TRISKAIDEKAPHOBIA
(Fear of the number 13)

No, I didn't make this one up.
This is really a phobia.

4. PANIC DISORDER

Have you ever had the horrible sensation that you're going to go crazy or die, but you neither go crazy nor die? That could be a panic attack. These can appear out of nowhere (for example, while you're taking a selfie) or when you're in an anxious state (for example, when there's turbulence on a plane). They can have different levels of intensity and different symptoms depending on the person, but I'm guessing that anyone who has suffered from them will agree with me that they are one of the most horrible things you can experience.

According to the *Diagnostic and Statistical Manual of Mental Disorders*, a panic attack is an "abrupt surge of intense fear or intense discomfort that reaches a peak within minutes, and during which time four or more of the following symptoms occur":

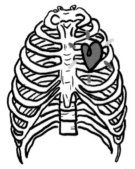

PALPITATIONS, POUNDING HEART, OR ACCELERATED HEART RATE

SWEATING

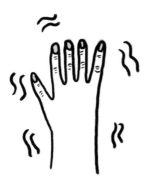

TREMBLING OR
SHAKING

SENSATION OF SHORTNESS
OF BREATH OR SMOTHERING

FEELING DIZZY, UNSTEADY,
LIGHT-HEADED, OR FAINT

NAUSEA OR
ABDOMINAL DISTRESS

CHILLS OR HOT
FLASHES

NUMBNESS OR
CHILLING SENSATION

FEELINGS OF
UNREALITY
(DEREALIZATION)

FEELING DETACHED FROM
ONESELF (DEPERSONALIZATION)

FEAR OF LOSING
CONTROL OR "GOING
CRAZY"

FEAR OF DYING

Panic disorder basically consists of having many panic attacks, just because and for no reason at all—out of nowhere or because you just saw a ghost—in a repeated fashion for at least a month. It also means existing constantly in a state of fear that you will have another panic attack.

5. GENERALIZED ANXIETY DISORDER (GAD)

Generalized anxiety disorder is characterized by the fact that those who suffer from it tend to live in a constant state of anxiety and worry that cannot be relieved by anything. It doesn't go away with prayers, or with essential oils, or with meditation (although meditation can help). It can't be cured with songs, or pleading, or kisses. The anxious person is usually unable to leave their worries aside and consequently begins to collect them, which often becomes unbearable to the point that concentration turns into an impossible task and sleep into something torturous. Aside from being accompanied by sleep disorders, GAD brings with it some other marvelous and not at all worrying symptoms (that's sarcasm) such as fatigue, irritability, and contractions or muscle pains.

ME WHEN I HEAR
THAT TEA IS GOOD
FOR ANXIETY

SURVIVAL GUIDE FOR THE ANXIOUS

Next you will find some tips, tricks, and coping strategies that will help you manage your anxiety (all are approved by me—an anxiety sufferer—and different therapists—anxiety professionals).

TALK ABOUT HOW YOU FEEL

An anxious person's superpower is seeming like they have everything under control while they are actually struggling with awful mental battles on the inside. Instead, let yourself feel, let yourself break down, let yourself lose control. Sometimes, the act of holding your emotions in for so long only makes the anxiety worse. So, go ahead and cry; talk to your friends. The simple act of being able to say "I'm feeling very anxious" can alleviate feelings of anxiety.

GO SEE A THERAPIST

It's easy to confuse stress with anxiety. Stress is the normal reaction our bodies and minds have when we have too much work or when we go through intense situations in our lives. This tends to disappear when we find the solution to said situations or when they come to an end. An anxiety disorder, on the other hand, manifests itself through fatalistic thoughts, the feeling of being incapable of stopping our brains from thinking, and physical exhaustion. When you feel that anxiety is starting to disrupt your day-to-day by making you feel terrible or because you're starting to avoid things, don't hesitate to consult a psychologist and/or psychiatrist.

Going to therapy is NOT bad. Taking medication is NOT bad if that's what a specialist thinks you need in order to get better. It does not mean you are weak, it doesn't translate to personal failure, it does not define you, it doesn't mean you are temporarily or perpetually broken. It just means you are listening to your body (in this case, your brain) and you are taking care of yourself.

Regarding the decision of taking medication, I personally was always very skeptical about psychiatric medication and thought that I could do it all alone. But I couldn't, and when I began my medicated treatment, I thanked the world and the geniuses at pharmaceutical companies for giving me the chance to feel better, to put an end to so much suffering, and to give myself the gift of feeling like myself again.

GIVE YOUR ANXIETY A NAME

Yes, this is a bit corny and a bit weird—not as weird as the time my psychologist made me buy a doll that looked like me, name her Amalita, and take care of her, play with her, speak to her, sleep with her, and even travel with her, but weird nonetheless.

Naming your anxiety will help you realize that:

- You are not your anxiety.
- Your anxiety is like a boring friend who can be annoying but who is harmless (for the most part).

P.S. Because I am not a psychologist, I am not up to date with the psycho-emotional sorcery behind the Amalita exercise, but I must say that it was wonderful for me and it helped me heal thousands of wounds. It also helped me realize that my girlfriend loves me for real, because when she'd get home, she would say hi to Amalita right after saying hi to me.

WRITE OR DRAW YOUR ANXIETY'S BIRTH CERTIFICATE HERE:

MIND THE FOUR PILLARS OF WELL-BEING

My psychiatrist says there are four pillars of well-being: taking your medication, exercising, getting good sleep,* and managing your stress. If these things are under control, your anxiety will be, too.

MEDITATE

Meditating is one of the best remedies for anxiety because it helps us calm our minds and live in the present. Be HERE and NOW. This exercise can be intimidating for many, but it's easier than it seems. You don't have to know how to meditate or need to have done it before. All you have to do is:

1. Find a place where you can enjoy some minutes of privacy. It can be your bedroom, your living room, or even your office bathroom.

2. Turn your cell phone to silent mode. You want to be undisturbed.

3. Sit in a comfortable place (it doesn't have to be the floor, you can sit on your favorite chair or on your couch).

---

* In my case, if I don't get enough sleep for more than two nights in a row, I basically go crazy. Nobody believes me when I say that not sleeping makes me feel worse than most people feel the morning after drinking an entire bottle of tequila, but it's true.

4. Start feeling your body—how it feels to have your back pressed to the chair, how your feet are touching the floor.

5. Close your eyes and focus on breathing. Take a deep breath in, let the air fill your lungs, and then exhale SLOWLY.

6. Focus on your breathing. If a thought comes in DON'T try to make it go away. Meditating is not about NOT thinking anything, but rather about letting the mind rest and just be.

7. If more thoughts come, just let them in and out. Meditating has its days. Some are great, some aren't. What matters is that you keep doing it. It's like exercising for the brain. The more you do it, the better it will feel.

8. Pay attention to how your body feels on the inside (sounds weird, I know, but it helps a lot).

9. Before opening your eyes again, try listening to the sounds around you, then move your fingers and toes a little. And then your hands and your feet. Then move your head slowly and begin regaining control of your body. When you feel ready, open your eyes.

Do this for five, ten, or twenty minutes a day and you will start experiencing the magic.

IN CASE OF A PANIC ATTACK

1. If you can, call somebody you trust and tell them how you're feeling.

2. Try to breathe deeply, or do this exercise: breathe in for four seconds (take your time), hold it for six, exhale slowly in eight seconds. Count while you are breathing in, holding, and breathing out. This will help your body relax.

3. If possible, go for a walk. Walking is a great way of feeling grounded, which alleviates the sense of impending panic.

4. Drink water.

5. Say to yourself the following words out loud: "I AM OK. I AM NOT IN A POSITION OF DANGER. I WILL NOT DIE OR GO CRAZY. THIS IS UNCOMFORTABLE BUT MOMENTARY. IT WILL COME TO AN END. I AM OK."

6. Practice the COLOR EXERCISE (I couldn't find a better name for this, I'm sorry).
   This exercise consists of taking your mind off the horrible symptoms of your panic attack and diverting your attention toward things that exist outside of you. You could do this with anything, but colors work very well for me. What I do is I start to look for things around me that are one specific color. For example: red things, yellow things, green things, or blue things. NEVER magenta things. Don't sabotage yourself like that.

KEEP A DIARY OF YOUR ANXIETY

Anxiety can be so overwhelming that it can seem to have no beginning or end. Writing about it can help you understand it a little better and, above all, help you understand what things or situations trigger it.

MAKE FRIENDS WITH YOUR ANXIETY

One of the things that makes everything worse is having anxiety about having anxiety. It can be difficult, but the ideal solution is finding a way to feel comfortable or calm during your anxious periods. Being able to say things like: "Yes, at this moment I have a lot of anxiety, this anxiety is terrifying and horrible, but it will pass and I'm going to be okay."

In order to get to this point, the best things you can do are:

Acknowledge your anxiety. Anxiety shrivels when we look it in the eye and gains power when we avoid it. Ignoring an anxiety disorder can start off inoffensive, but if left to grow, it can cause your well-being to deteriorate in a drastic and dramatic way. You may start by avoiding crossing the street, but that can turn into never leaving your home, and then no longer seeing your friends, and so forth, until everything explodes.

Laugh about your anxiety. It's difficult, but it can also be pretty funny. The only thing you have to do to die of laughter is google "anxiety memes" and smile.

PRACTICE BEING KIND TO YOURSELF

God knows that us anxious people have the power to be extra hard on ourselves, to ask too much of ourselves, to think that we could have always done things better or differently. Repeat the following phrases to yourself:

I'M NOT BROKEN. ACTUALLY, YES, I'M A LITTLE BROKEN, BUT I'M INCREDIBLE AND I DESERVE ALL THE BEST.

I'M ENOUGH JUST THE WAY I AM.
I'M NOT MISSING ANYTHING.
I'M NOT TOO MUCH OF ANYTHING.

THERE'S NO NEED TO FEAR ONE BAD DAY A YEAR.

Write down your own phrase here:

_____

_____

_____

_____

_____

_____

_____

_____

_____

_____

_____

_____

_____

_____

SUPPORT GROUP

ALBERTO MONTT

CHAPTER 5

WHAT BRINGS YOU DOWN CAN SAVE YOU

FEAR, BEING ANTICIPATORY, IS ALWAYS
WITHOUT KNOWLEDGE. IT IS A MENTAL
CALCULATION BASED ON THE FUTURE
UNKNOWN....... BRAVERY IS ALWAYS
MORE INTELLIGENT THAN FEAR, SINCE
IT IS BUILT ON THE FOUNDATION OF WHAT
ONE KNOWS ABOUT ONESELF: THE
KNOWLEDGE OF ONE'S STRENGTH AND
CAPACITY, OF ONE'S PASSION.
　　　　　—Letter to Vincent Van Gogh

NICOLE KRAUSS
Writer
Genius
Afraid of death

It's okay to be filled with fear. We all are. In fact, we are probably more afraid now than we were when we were kids and thought there were monsters under our beds. Growing up is scary, very much so. I live in fear that everything in my fridge is going to poison and kill me, and most of the phone calls I make to my mom are to ask her if I can eat the meat that's been in the freezer for five months or the ham that expired two days ago.

We are filled with fear because we live in a society that tells us what we need to be like through social media—through inspirational phrases, granola, and perfect, YouTube-tutorial-worthy makeup. There's nothing wrong with all-natural granola, but it isn't a prerequisite for being happy or being okay.

We live in a society that systematically works to oppress and hide all things that challenge its order. It's okay to be sad as long as you don't talk about it. It's okay to be gay as long as it isn't noticeable. The same thing happens with heartbreak, with frustration, with hopelessness, and with fear. Especially with fear.

But all that oppression, all that silence, piles up and turns us into an army of the emotionally damaged, a collection of people who are anxious and afraid.

We have to speak out. We have to make the things that are invisible seen. We have to make some people uncomfortable in order to help free ourselves. We need to shout: it's okay to be imperfect, it's okay to be a little broken. It's okay not to be okay. It's okay to be afraid.

FEAR SAVES YOU

Fear saves us. Literally. It exists in order to save our lives, so instead of thinking of it as something we have to get rid of completely, it's time to show it some gratitude.

Here are a few examples of fear playing the part of a lifesaver.

FEAR OF HEIGHTS
(OR THAT SMALL VOID YOU
FEEL EVERY TIME YOU LOOK
DOWN FROM A HIGH BALCONY)

Saves you from falling to
your death

FEAR OF EMOTIONAL PAIN

Saves you from going out with
the wrong people, who you can
identify because they tell lies,
have another boyfriend or girlfriend
behind your back, or don't like French
fries or pizza (this is simply offensive).

FEAR OF ELEVATORS

Saves you from having to pay a gym membership

FEAR OF CLOWNS

Saves you from going to birthday parties you don't want to attend or having to lie in order to get out of one.

LIST OF THINGS I DID THANKS TO MY FEAR

> Wrote this book.

> Sent a text to a girl and asked her out.

> Spoke in front of more than three hundred people.

> Quit a job that was making me unhappy.

> Learned how to cook (for fear of dying of hunger).

> Got on a plane (for fear of not visiting new places).

> Got to know new streets in my neighborhood (as a way to avoid large avenues).

LIST OF THINGS YOU HAVE DONE THANKS TO YOUR FEAR

> _____
> _____
> _____

> _____
> _____

> _____

> _____

> _____
> _____

> _____

> _____

> _____

SUPPORT GROUP

NICO GONZÁLEZ

A FRIEND TOLD ME
THAT BEING AFRAID IS OK
BUT YOU SHOULD
NEVER BE A COWARD.

FEAR IS
THE OPPOSITE
OF LOVE.
AND LOVE
IS BEING BRAVE.

DON'T LET
FEAR STOP YOU.
WE ARE ALL HERE
WITH YOU.

WHEN FEAR IS AN OBSTACLE,
IT MUST BE TRANSFORMED INTO ENTHUSIASM
IN THE DESIRE TO DO THINGS.

A BRIEF GUIDE TO OVERCOMING YOUR FEARS

Or, exercises that will help make fear your best friend.

1. SAY GOODBYE TO EMOTIONAL HYPOCHONDRIA

Hypochondria, in its most literal sense, is the irrational conviction that you are gravely ill, based on a constant suspicion that is in turn a product of endless self-analyses that you perform on your body. It never fails to yield catastrophic results.

It means living in an endless state of panic, where a piercing pain in your left eye is actually glaucoma, feeling very thirsty is a sure symptom of type 2 diabetes, and a migraine is the sign of an aneurysm—one that, if it doesn't kill you first, will surely leave you debilitated forever.

Emotional hypochondria functions in the same way, but on the feelings level. It is when we start thinking alarmist thoughts and doubting everything, analyzing and overanalyzing every situation, and always expecting the worst and expecting our worst fears to come true.

What follows are a few illustrated examples of this, as well as how to fight them.

CASE NUMBER 1

I really like Lola. But I sent her a text three minutes ago and got no response at all. Surely, she doesn't like me, and even if she does like me she's going to break my heart like my ex did. I'd rather step on a Lego than have my heart broken again. I probably shouldn't speak to her anymore. I should delete all my social media. I'm going to die alone and a born-again virgin. When I die, you can write on my gravestone: "She wanted to be happy but failed because she chose never to look for love again after the day Lola didn't text her back."

DIAGNOSIS: Fear of loneliness, fear of rejection, fear of being vulnerable.

THE CURE: Stop generalizing bad experiences. Wait more than three minutes for somebody to text you back.

CASE NUMBER 2

My boss told me, "We need to talk." I'm sure that he is going to fire me and tell me that I have no talent. I'm going to have to begin a career as a dog walker. Not that that's a bad thing, but what if one day while I'm walking the dogs in the park, I fall asleep and one of the dogs chews my face off, and then I have to get a face transplant and I'm left with a dead person's face?

DIAGNOSIS: Fear of failure, fear of mutilation, fear of unemployment.

THE CURE: Don't get ahead of yourself. Hear what the boss has to say before you begin to worry. Give the dog enough food. Trust in yourself. Don't forget that failure is just as important as success.

CASE NUMBER 3

Draw yourself here →

Write down your case here →

_____

_____

_____

_____

_____

DIAGNOSIS: _____

THE CURE: _____

2. PRACTICE PROGRESSIVE UNLEARNING

Due to the fact that many of our fears are learned (see the example of my aunt María Eugenia's poodle on page 45), we have the ability to unlearn them. How? By confronting them head-on, with determination (even if your legs are trembling and you want to run away).

In order to prevent this task from turning into complete agony, confront ONLY one fear at a time and take all the time you need. ALL THE TIME. Your whole life, if necessary.

Use the following graph to classify your fears from least to greatest and come up with a reward system for yourself for every fear you're able to confront.

FEARS

LEVEL OF FEAR
(FROM 0 TO 1000, I WOULD RATHER
DIE THAN FACE THIS)

ANTI-FEAR REWARD TABLE

FEAR CONFRONTED	REWARD

3. FAKE IT TILL YOU MAKE IT

For this exercise, the trick is to pretend you have things under control until you actually do. Fool your brain and tell it: "This is not scary to you. You are super brave. You can do this," during moments when you're filled with panic and have the desire to call it quits on the entire day and get in bed for a full month.

At first, your brain will feel confused (kind of like when the person you have a crush on likes twenty of your posts on Instagram but then leaves you on read over text for three days), and it will be uncomfortable and not very effective, but with time and practice this can become so effective that one day, you might wake up having overcome your fear, or at least having put a serious dent in it.

4. CREATE A LIST OF COURAGEOUS ACTIONS

This exercise is an invitation to stop with the negativity and constant malicious criticism we direct toward ourselves. Instead of focusing on what we do wrong, on the things we've avoided because of fear, the task here is to write down at least three courageous things you accomplish throughout the course of the day. You'll soon discover there are many more of them than you'd thought. Courage isn't necessarily equivalent to a heroic act out of an action movie (for example, rescuing an old lady from being run over by a truck and dying), but rather can be made up of simple actions such as crossing the street (if you're afraid of crossing streets), paying a bill on time, saying NO to things you would say yes to only out of obligation, waiting in line at the bank, hitting "send" on that email you've been doubting for so long, and confronting your personal monsters on a daily basis, whether they're larger monsters like loneliness or smaller monsters like finding a stray hair in your McFlurry.

BRAVERY AWARD FOR
CROSSING THE WIDEST
AVENUE IN THE CITY

Write down your own list of brave actions here:

_____

_____

_____

_____

_____

_____

_____

_____

_____

_____

_____

_____

_____

_____

5. CREATE AN "IN CASE OF EMERGENCY" CARD

In case of paralysis or an emergency situation, cut out this card and give it to one of your friends, so they will know what to do.*

* My friends always know what works best for me, which basically consists of saying one of the following phrases: "Amalia, I promise you that this isn't the case," and "Malita, you can do this," and "You survived growing up in a country governed by Pablo Escobar. You got this, *mija*."

6. AS ROXETTE WOULD SAY, "LISTEN TO YOUR HEART"

The best tools to fight your fears are already inside you, and these are your intuition and your dreams.

INTUITION

My theory is that fear distances us from intuition, and therein lies its "power." Intuition—or, as I like to call it, "the voice that speaks to me when I'm doing things right"—is infinitely wiser than fear. Always try to summon it and take its advice when fear comes knocking on your door.

DREAMS

We are made out of dreams—dreams nurture us, they outline a path for us, they point us in a direction. Dreams save us, they pick us up when we fall down, they give us a PURPOSE. When fear shows up, remember that dreams (just like love) can suffer through anything, can believe anything, can wait for anything, can withstand anything. Dreams will never cease to be.

7. PLAY THE MOVIE IN YOUR HEAD

This sounds like crazy advice. I know. I thought so, too, the first time my therapist told me about it. But here is the thing: fear and anxiety are so powerful, that once they are sparked in us, a movie starts to play, and it's a horror movie with an ending we don't like—that is, if we can imagine the ending.

Naturally, what we do is shut the movie down because we fear it's going to come true. For example, this happens when you are on a plane and it hits turbulence. The movie quickly starts playing in your head: the plane is crashing and you are going to die. You don't want to even have this thought in your head (fear makes us very superstitious), but there's a catch to this. The more you shut that movie down, the more your fear grows, because you are not facing it, you are running from it. And fear feeds on fear.

A plane is maybe not the best place to do this exercise if you are afraid of planes, but you can try it in a safe place where you feel calm and grounded. Let the movie of your fear play in your head. You don't have to get to the ending right away. You can try different times until you get to see the credits. And while you are at it, BEAT IT. Beat your fear in your imagination (but if you don't that is okay). The purpose of this exercise is 1.) to expose yourself to your fear and stop feeding it and 2.) to get you to the bottom of it so you can understand it. Can you see yourself beating your fear? What is REALLY at the end of the movie?

8. GATHER THE FACTS

One of the easiest, simplest ways of punching fear in the face REAL HARD is reading a lot of information about whatever it is that you fear.

As I am writing this, I have already faced three mini panic attacks around the possibility of having COVID-19 and dying alone in a hospital far away from the people I love. This is a sensible matter, I know. And I also know that is a fear many of us will share until there is a vaccine and this paragraph feels like something from the past (which honestly, I can't wait to happen). Until then, there is one thing that helps me get by: knowing the numbers. Knowing what I need to do to be safe, and making sure I'm doing so. Knowing how the disease works, what I need to do to prevent it, what it would look like if I got it.

Knowing the facts helps you manage the lack of control that fear enjoys so much. It gives you the tools and knowledge for you to either beat fear or be prepared for it.

9. SET YOURSELF TO WIN

This I learned from professional athletes. Before a race, for example, BMX athletes play the whole event in their heads (this exercise is a cousin of the "play the movie in your head" one). They imagine every jump, every roller, everything until the finish line. They know how they are going to do every move (because they have practiced), and at the end they win.

Set yourself to win. If you are afraid of public speaking, for example, imagine the whole thing first. How would you do it? What do you need to be successful at it? You will need calm. Practice meditation. Practice the whole thing in your head (and outside of your head, if you can). Visualize yourself winning and you will win. Now, remember that winning is not the same thing as something being easy or enjoyable. It might still be hard, but you will succeed at it, and the more you do, the more power and confidence you will have in yourself (and the less the fear will be present).

I know you're afraid, but being afraid is all right, because didn't anybody ever tell you fear is a superpower? Fear can make you faster and cleverer and stronger.....If you're very wise and very strong, fear doesn't have to make you cruel or cowardly. Fear can make you kind. It doesn't matter if there's nothing under the bed or in the dark, so long as you know it's okay to be afraid of it.....You're always going to be afraid, even if you learn to hide it. Fear is like a companion, a constant companion, always there. But that's okay, because fear can bring us together. Fear can bring you home.

— CLARA OSWALD
on *Doctor Who*

"Listen" (Season 8, Episode 4)

SUPPORT GROUP

CATALINA
BU

LOSING MY
MEMORY

BY CATALINA BU

APPENDIX A

FEAR AND WRITING

Fear and writing are the same thing. The only difference is that we were born ready for the first one, and not for the second (and in fact, we are never actually ready to write—that's why every book is a leap in the dark from the top of a very tall mountain with Virginia Woolf's voice yelling in the background, "Friend, NO!"*). Both things require creativity and imagination as their main ingredients.

For example, what would telling a story about our fear of airplanes be like without creativity? Maybe something like this: "The plane will crash. I will likely die. The end." This isn't even a good story, and it doesn't resemble fear or anxiety in the slightest (especially NOT anxiety).

But with creativity and even the slightest bit of turbulence that feels to us like the end of the world, we get a different story: "The plane is going to become detached from the magical magnets that

---

* Translation: Friend, don't even think about trying. I survived miraculously. In fact, I didn't really survive. Look for a better role model.

hold it up in the sky and we are going to plummet down. Would I have a heart attack while freefalling? I feel like I'm having a heart attack now. What if the plane crashes and I survive? I don't want to have to eat human flesh. What would human flesh taste like? And what if we fall and I do die? How is my mother going to feel? Would my ex-girlfriend go to the funeral? Please don't let her go to my funeral. I should have written down my will. Would the accident be covered by the papers? Would they write a headline along the lines of: 'WRITER WHO WAS AFRAID OF FLYING DIES IN A PLANE CRASH—YOUR WORST FEARS DO COME TRUE'? I think that's a pretty good headline, I'm going to jot it down if this plane doesn't crash. What will I feel at the time of my death? Am I really going to die on an airplane? Am I really asking myself all these questions?"

As said by writer Karen Thompson Walker in her TED Talk "What Fear Can Teach Us," fear and writing (or stories, rather) have the same structure:

A character (us); a plot consisting of a beginning, a middle, and an end (I write an email to my friend in which I tell her everything I feel for the person I am secretly and hopelessly in love with, my cat then decides to play on my desk and accidentally sends the email/confession to half my contacts, and included in that list of people is the person I am secretly in love with who I refer to in said email as THE LOVE OF MY LIFE FOREVER); vivid imagery (the beautiful but sometimes demonic cat decides to step on my computer right that instant when he usually never stands there thanks to the spray I use to discipline animals that smells like eucalyptus, which I bought with the person I am secretly in love with—then, after the email has been sent, I decide to do research online for about an hour: HOW TO TAKE BACK A SENT EMAIL. The next hour, research: HOW TO KNOW IF SOMEONE HAS READ YOUR EMAIL. And the one after that: HOW TO HACK A GMAIL ACCOUNT, HOW TO

ESCAPE FROM THE COUNTRY IN UNDER A DAY, HOW TO CHANGE MY IDENTITY FOREVER).

As I was creating this book, while my fear of writing about fear had me submerged in a state of total frustration and despair, I discovered that the good thing about writing and fear being almost the same thing is that we can stop seeing fear as a threat or a small tragedy that we have to carry around with us, and instead start celebrating it as a powerful act of creativity and healing.

Write down the story of your own fears. Take a leap of faith (I promise, it's a powerful and liberating experience that has surprising results).

THE STORY OF MY FEARS

BY _____
(WRITE YOUR NAME HERE)

_____

_____

_____

_____

_____

_____

_____

_____

_____

_____

_____

_____

APPENDIX B

SURVIVAL AND SUPPORT GUIDE FOR THE ANXIOUS PERSON'S FRIENDS AND FAMILY

Counting on support and understanding from the people we love is FUNDAMENTAL to the emotional and mental well-being of any person with anxiety. And so, dear loved ones, this guide is for you.

YOUR FRIEND/PARTNER/ COLLEAGUE IS NOT EXAGGERATING

Our society does not give mental health the attention it deserves. This is why, when someone tells us: "I don't feel okay enough to go out, I'm feeling very nervous (or whatever it is)," we tend to think that they're exaggerating and that the only thing they need is to be lectured and told to stop complaining and get out of the house.

THIS IS NOT TRUE. Feeling unwell because of anxiety is the same as or worse than feeling unwell because of chronic bronchitis. We need to give mental health its true dimension and acknowledge that it takes special care and treatment to get better.

This is also a good time to remember that you should never tell someone to stop taking their medication because "they are strong enough and don't need it," because taking mental health medication is for "the weak," or for any other reason.

Would you ever tell a diabetic person not to take their insulin? NO. Let's all end the stigma around antidepressant or antianxiety medications by understanding that they can be a vital resource in someone's path to well-being.

LISTEN

Usually, it's very difficult to let ourselves accept that we have a mental health issue, and it becomes even harder to talk about it with someone else. If someone you trust confides in you enough to talk about it, listen to them without judgment, give them a big hug, and let them know that you are there for them. You can also ask them how can you be of help. Try to understand their anxiety. What triggers it (if they know, because sometimes we don't)? How can you be supportive at all times? What can you do in case an anxiety or panic attack occurs?

The best ways to cope with anxiety sometimes seem counterintuitive. This makes me think of a video in which Kendall Jenner tells her sister Kylie she is having a major anxiety attack about stepping onto the Met Gala red carpet. Kylie's response is to ask Kendall for help because she has no idea which high heels she should wear.

At first sight, it looks as if Kylie is being the worst person on the planet by blatantly ignoring her sister's very urgent feelings in the most horrible self-centered way. But you know what? Kylie is actually being THE BEST SISTER OF THEM ALL. She is trying to distract Kendall by refocusing her attention on anything other than her anxiety (i.e., the high heels dilemma). This shows compassion, empathy, and a profound understanding of her sister's anxiety. Now, everybody's anxiety is different. That's why asking what to do and what not to do is so important, and really, the best way you can help

ACTIVATE YOUR POWERS OF PATIENCE AND UNDERSTANDING

Anxious people are a little weird. That's the wonderful—and sometimes difficult—thing about us. Often, our own minds refuse to stop spinning, so please know that:

- We tend to cancel plans at the last minute. Not because we want to, but because we really can't go out, or we really aren't feeling okay.

- We can be very bad at answering texts, emails, calls, or letters delivered by carrier pigeon. Love us regardless. Please. This can happen because we get easily overwhelmed.
- At times, we will need a certain thing and then, five minutes later, need the exact opposite.

DO NOT SAY THE FOLLOWING THINGS — EVER

YOU CAN DO IT ALL

No. If we could do it all we would have stopped our brains from spinning a loooong time ago.

YOU ARE STRONGER THAN YOUR ANXIETY

Yes and no. We know this in the bottom of our hearts, but this isn't helpful during an anxious episode and will instead make us feel weaker.

JUST TRY TO RELAX

PLEASE DO NOT EVER SAY THIS. Having anxiety basically means being unable to relax. For example, my friends who saw that I was very stressed-out while writing this book asked me: "Amalia, do you want a relaxing massage for your birthday?" To which I responded: "No. Massages stress me out." They responded: "So then what makes you feel good?" Me: "Spending the entire day in my bed, reading in my pajamas."

And so their gift to me was an incredibly soft blanket, some lemon verbena tea, a set of eight-hundred-thread-count sheets, and a Virginia Woolf novel.

MAKE DECISIONS

Sometimes, it can be difficult for anxious people to make decisions because our heads begin to doubt everything and think about whether or not we made the right choice. And about how, if we didn't, we're going to live with that uncertainty for the rest of our lives.

And so, if it's time to eat and you ask us what we want and we respond: "I don't know, whatever you choose." PLEASE MAKE THE DECISION. THANK YOU.

ACKNOWLEDGMENTS

It takes a lot of people to make a book. I want to thank Andrea Montejo, Meg Leder, Amy Sun, Shannon Kelly, Patrick Nolan, Santiago Andrade, Amanda Arango, Hugo J. Andrade, Julian Camacho, Alejandra Algorta, Gloria Susana Esquivel, Alejandro Gomez Dugand, Maria Luque, Power Paola, Herikita, Milena Hachim, Alberto Montt, Catalina Bu, Nico Gonzalez, Brenda Lozano, Marcel Ventura, Andrea Loeber, and Carolina Lopez for helping this book come to life with your talent, patience, and infinite wisdom. All of you make me believe that love is truly stronger than fear. I want to thank Jessica Kisner for forcing me to cross Atlantic Avenue multiple times back in 2015, but at the same time taking the long way home when I felt I couldn't.

Finally, I want to thank Nela Gonzalez for taking my hand and waking with me to the other side of my biggest terrors. Thank you for turning on the light.

SUPPORT GROUP CONTRIBUTORS

María Luque is a graphic designer from Argentina. Her book *La mano del pintor* is an absolute marvel. Besides drawing prodigiously, María has very beautiful glasses and a great sense of humor.

@maria.j.luque

marialuque.bigcartel.com

Alejandro Gómez-Dugand is the chief editor of Colombian independent magazine *Cerosetenta*. He studied literature but started working as a journalist before he graduated from university. He hates big crowds. Like me, he also hates vomiting.

@gomezdugand

cerosetenta.com

Power Paola is a visual artist, illustrator, and storyteller. She's the author of books such as *Virus Tropical*, *La madre monte*, and *Todo va a estar bien* (Everything Will Be Okay), which is an incredible title that I would have loved to use on this book.

@powerpaola

Alejandra Algorta is a writer and editor. She was born in Bogotá in a tub on an early Wednesday in 1991 before the doctor came. Since then, her body only wants to return to the water. She got the first mention in the IV Premio Barco de Vapor award for her book *Pez quiere ir al mar* and recently published her first novel *nuncaseolvida* with Babel. She is the founder and editor of the poetry publishing house Cardumen.

@acercandra_

Gloria Susana Esquivel is a writer and poet who hosts a podcast called *Womansplaining* where she explores feminism in today's world. Her first novel, *Animals at the End of the World*, will be published by the University of Texas Press in spring 2020. She hates airplanes and is afraid of heights.

@gloriasusanaesquivel

juradopormadonna.tumblr.com

Milena Hachim, better known as Milo, is my Instagram friend and one of my favorite illustrators. She lives in Santiago de Chile, likes *Stranger Things*, and has the ability to design the most beautiful pins in the world.

@milohachim

milohachim.com

Alberto Montt is a graphic designer and illustrator, who was born in Ecuador (which is something I learned while writing this mini biography), and in my heart, he is one of my favorite people from Chile. You may know him from his comic strip *Dosis diarias* of brilliant and famous vignettes. I know him as the human being who responds to everything I say with: "NERD."

@albertomontt

dosisdiarias.com

Nico González is an illustrator and excellent cartoonist from Chile. He has had a pencil in hand ever since he's had a conscience. My favorite drawing of his is one he made of Selena, which I infamously attempted to copy in this book.

@holanicogonzalez

Catalina Bu—better known as La Cata—is the author of *Diario de un solo* (Volumes 1 and 2), books I always turn to when I need to feel happy. She's a great illustrator, friend, and mom to Moño, her dog.

@catalinabu

catalinabu.com

SHARE YOUR FEARS WITH ME!

WEB:

www.amaliaandrade.com

TWITTER:

@amaliaandrade_

INSTAGRAM:

@amaliaandrade_

AMALIA ANDRADE was born in Cali, Colombia, in 1986. She studied literature at Pontifical Xavierian University in Bogotá. She's been drawing forever. She's written for several magazines in both Colombia and the United States. She believes strongly in the power of keeping a diary. When she grows up, she wants to be a mix between Sylvia Plath and Tina Fey. She lives in Bogotá with her cats and is the author of *You Always Change the Love of Your Life (for Another Love or Another Life)*.

You Always Change the Love of Your Life (for Another Love or Another Life)

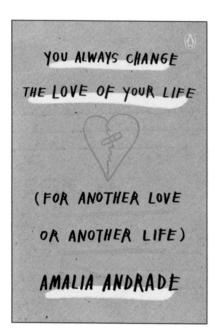

When Amalia Andrade was faced with her own heartbreak, she knew she couldn't let herself get lost in despair. So she constructed the ultimate first-aid kit: an interactive guide to getting over someone through reflections, recipes, and lots of ingenious ideas for transforming a negative experience into a liberating one. In *You Always Change the Love of Your Life*, she reveals the secret to mending your heart and maybe even opening it up again.

"Andrade feels like one of your friends, but not like she's got it all figured out. . . . It's easy to believe that she knows what true heartbreak feels like." –*Lambda Literary*